CLASSICS Illustrated®

Nathaniel Hawthorne
THE HOUSE OF THE SEVEN GABLES

essay by
Joshua Miller, M.Phil.
Columbia University

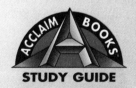

ACCLAIM BOOKS

STUDY GUIDE

.CLASSICS.
Illustrated®

The House of the Seven Gables
Originally published as Classics Illustrated no. 52

Art by George Woodbridge
Adaption by J. O'Rourke
Cover by Chuck Wotjkiewicz

For Classics Illustrated Study Guides
computer recoloring by Colorgraphix
editor: Madeleine Robins
assistant editor: Gregg Sanderson
design: Joseph Caponsacco

Dale-Chall R.L.: 8.4

ISBN 1-57840-041-4

Acclaim Books, New York, NY
Printed in the United States

THE HOUSE OF THE SEVEN GABLES

By Nathaniel Hawthorne

HALF-WAY DOWN A BY-STREET OF A NEW ENGLAND TOWN STANDS A RUSTY WOODEN HOUSE, WITH SEVEN ACUTELY PEAKED GABLES FACING TOWARDS VARIOUS POINTS OF THE COMPASS, AND A HUGE, CLUSTERED CHIMNEY IN THE MIDST.

THE STREET IS PYNCHEON STREET; THE HOUSE IS THE OLD PYNCHEON HOUSE; AND AN ELM TREE OF WIDE CIRCUMFERENCE, ROOTED BEFORE IT, IS FAMILIAR TO EVERY TOWN-BORN CHILD BY THE TITLE OF THE PYNCHEON ELM.

PYNCHEON STREET FORMERLY BORE THE HUMBLER TITLE OF MAULE'S LANE, FROM THE NAME OF THE ORIGINAL OCCUPANT OF THE SOIL, MATTHEW MAULE.

BUT IN THE GROWTH OF THE PURITAN SETTLEMENT, THE SITE BECAME DESIRABLE TO THE PROMINENT AND POWERFUL COLONEL PYNCHEON, WHO CLAIMED IT ON THE STRENGTH OF A GRANT FROM THE LEGISLATURE.

SATAN TAKE THEE, COLONEL PYNCHEON! THY CLAIM DOST NOT COVER MY HUMBLE GARDEN-GROUND AND HOMESTEAD.

THE DISPUTE CAME TO AN END WITH THE DEATH OF MATTHEW MAULE, WHO, IN THE TERRIBLE MADNESS THAT GRIPPED NEW ENGLAND A FEW YEARS LATER, WAS EXECUTED FOR WITCHCRAFT.

'TIS COLONEL PYNCHEON'S DOING! I AM HOUNDED TO DEATH FOR MY LAND.

IT IS TRUE THAT COLONEL PYNCHEON HAD WITH SPECIAL ZEAL SOUGHT THE CONDEMNATION OF MATTHEW MAULE. AT THE MOMENT OF EXECUTION...

GOD WILL GIVE HIM BLOOD TO DRINK!

AFTER MAULE'S DEATH, THE HUMBLE HOMESTEAD FELL INTO COLONEL PYNCHEON'S GRASP. IT WAS SOON LEARNED THAT THE COLONEL WAS TO ERECT A FAMILY MANSION ON THE SOIL.

THE COLONEL BUILDS HIS HOUSE OVER AN UNQUIET GRAVE.

BUT THE OLD PURITAN WAS NOT A MAN TO BE TURNED ASIDE BY A CORPSE. HE EVEN HIRED, AS HEAD CARPENTER, THE SON OF THE MAN FROM WHOSE GRIP THE SOIL HAD BEEN WRESTED.

'TIS STRANGE HOW TOM MAULE SERVES HIS FATHER'S DEADLY ENEMY.

WHEN THE GREAT HOUSE OF THE SEVEN GABLES WAS READY, COLONEL PYNCHEON BADE ALL THE TOWN TO BE HIS GUESTS. THITHER THEY CAME, DRAWN BY CURIOSITY AND THE RICH SCENT OF MEAT AND FOWLS THAT BELCHED FORTH FROM THE KITCHEN CHIMNEY.

INSIDE THE HOUSE, A STRANGE CIRCUMSTANCE WAS NOTED. COLONEL PYNCHEON WAS NOWHERE VISIBLE.

SURELY THE FOUNDER OF THIS STATELY MANSION SHOULD STAND IN HIS OWN HALL TO OFFER FIRST WELCOME TO HIS VISITORS.

THE HEIRS OF COLONEL PYNCHEON CAME INTO A RICH ESTATE, WHICH ESTATE, WHICH INCLUDED A CLAIM THROUGH AN INDIAN DEED TO A VAST TRACT OF EASTERN LANDS.

IT WOULD HAVE BEEN THE SOURCE OF INCALCULABLE WEALTH, BUT THE PYNCHEONS WERE NEVER ABLE TO VALIDATE THE CLAIM.

IF YOUR FATHER, THE COLONEL, HAD BUT LIVED A FEW WEEKS LONGER, HE MIGHT HAVE DONE ALL THAT WOULD BE NECESSARY TO RENDER THE CLAIM ACCEPTABLE. BUT NOW SOMETHING IS LACKING, AND THERE IS NOTHING YOU CAN DO ABOUT IT.

GENERATIONS CAME AND PASSED. FROM FATHER TO SON, THE PYNCHEONS CLUNG TO THEIR ANCESTRAL HOME. THE FOUNDER'S PORTRAIT, IN OBEDIENCE, IT WAS SAID, TO A PROVISION OF HIS WILL, REMAINED AFFIXED TO THE WALL OF THE ROOM IN WHICH HE DIED.

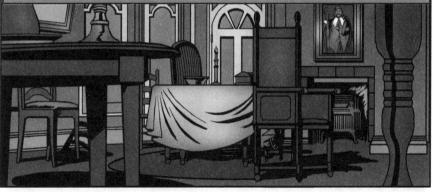

THE POPULAR IMAGINATION DID NOT FORGET MATTHEW MAULE'S CURSE. MANY YEARS LATER, THE SUDDEN DEATH OF ANOTHER PYNCHEON WAS FELT TO GIVE ADDITIONAL PROOF OF ITS POWER.

'TIS HOW THE OLD COLONEL DIED.

THE PYNCHEONS LIVED FOR MORE THAN 150 YEARS, AND MAULE'S CURSE REMAINED A PART OF THE FAMILY INHERITANCE. IF A PYNCHEON DID BUT CLEAR HIS THROAT.

HE HAS MAULE'S BLOOD TO DRINK.

ABOUT THIRTY YEARS BEFORE THE ACTION OF OUR STORY COMMENCES, THE PRINCIPAL HOLDER OF THE PYNCHEON WEALTH MET A VIOLENT DEATH—OR SO IT WAS ADJUDGED.

THE MASTER HAS BEEN MURDERED!

A YOUNG NEPHEW, CLIFFORD PYNCHEON, WAS CONVICTED OF THE CRIME. AT THE TIME OF OUR STORY, HE STILL LANGUISHED IN PRISON, ALTHOUGH THERE HAD LATELY BEEN RUMORS THAT HE WAS SOON TO BE RELEASED FROM HIS LIVING TOMB.

ANOTHER NEPHEW, JAFFREY PYNCHEON, WHOSE TESTIMONY HELPED CONVICT CLIFFORD, BECAME HEIR TO THE PYNCHEON FORTUNE UPON HIS UNCLE'S DEATH. HE WAS NOW A JUDGE, AND UNQUESTIONABLY A CREDIT TO HIS RACE.

HEPZIBAH, A SISTER OF THE UNFORTUNATE CLIFFORD, NOW DWELT IN THE HOUSE OF THE SEVEN GABLES, IN WHICH SHE HAD A LIFE ESTATE BY THE WILL OF HER UNCLE. SHE WAS WRETCHEDLY POOR.

THE LAST AND YOUNGEST OF THE PYNCHEONS WAS A COUNTRY COUSIN NAMED PHOEBE.

AS FOR MATTHEW MAULE, HIS LINE WAS BELIEVED TO BE EXTINCT. THERE WAS NO RECORD ANYWHERE OF ANY OF HIS DESCENDANTS. AND NOW—IN A VERY HUMBLE WAY, AS WILL BE SEEN — WE PROCEED TO OPEN OUR NARRATIVE.

It STILL LACKED HALF AN HOUR OF SUNRISE, WHEN, IN THE HOUSE OF THE SEVEN GABLES, HEPZIBAH PYNCHEON AROSE FROM HER SOLITARY PILLOW. WHEN SHE HAD DRESSED, SHE TOOK FROM A DESK A SMALL PORTRAIT AND GAZED FONDLY UPON IT.

It WAS THE LIKENESS OF A YOUNG MAN, WITH FULL, TENDER LIPS AND BEAUTIFUL EYES.

Brushing ASIDE A TEAR, HEPZIBAH DESCENDED THE STAIRS AND ENTERED THE PARLOR. FOR A LONG MOMENT SHE STOOD, AS IF IN REVERENCE, BEFORE THE ANCIENT PORTRAIT ON THE WALL.

Then SHE WENT TO A ROOM BENEATH THE GABLE FRONTING THE STREET. HERE SHE HAD FITTED UP A SHOP, WHICH SHE WOULD OPEN TODAY TO THE PUBLIC.

Poverty HAD COME UP WITH HER AT LAST. THE MISTRESS OF THE HOUSE OF THE SEVEN GABLES HAD TO EARN HER OWN FOOD OR STARVE.

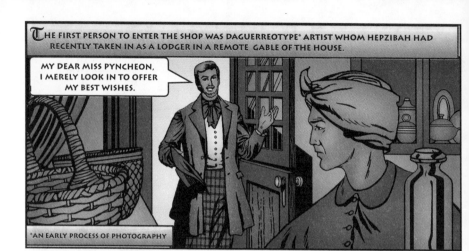

THE FIRST PERSON TO ENTER THE SHOP WAS DAGUERREOTYPE* ARTIST WHOM HEPZIBAH HAD RECENTLY TAKEN IN AS A LODGER IN A REMOTE GABLE OF THE HOUSE.

MY DEAR MISS PYNCHEON, I MERELY LOOK IN TO OFFER MY BEST WISHES.

*AN EARLY PROCESS OF PHOTOGRAPHY

AH, MR. HOLGRAVE, I NEVER CAN GO THROUGH WITH IT! I AM TOO OLD, TOO FEEBLE! AND TO THINK THAT A BORN LADY SHOULD BE REDUCED TO RUNNING A SHOP!

I DON'T THINK ANY LADY OF YOUR FAMILY HAS EVER DONE A MORE HEROIC THING SINCE THIS HOUSE WAS BUILT, THAN YOU ARE DOING IN IT TODAY.

IF THE PYNCHEONS HAD ALWAYS ACTED SO NOBLY, I DOUBT IF OLD MAULE'S CURSE, OF WHICH YOU TOLD ME ONCE, WOULD HAVE HAD MUCH WEIGHT WITH GOD.

IF MAULE'S GHOST, OR A DESCENDANT OF HIS, COULD SEE ME NOW, HE WOULD BE WELL PLEASED.

WHEN HOLGRAVE HAD GONE, TWO TOWNSMEN STOPPED BY THE WINDOW.

HERE'S A SIGHT! OLD MAID PYNCHEON IS SETTING UP A SHOP!

SHE'LL NEVER MAKE IT GO. HER FACE IS ENOUGH TO FRIGHTEN THE DEVIL HIMSELF, IF HE HAD A MIND TO TRADE WITH HER.

A LITTLE LATER, HEPZIBAH HAD HER FIRST CUSTOMER.

I WANT THAT GINGERBREAD MAN IN THE WINDOW—THE ONE THAT HAS NOT THE BROKEN FOOT.

HEPZIBAH GAVE IT TO HIM.

NO MATTER FOR THE MONEY. YOU ARE WELCOME TO THE GINGERBREAD.

A FEW MINUTES LATER, THE BOY RETURNED.

WHAT IS IT NOW, CHILD?

I WANT THAT OTHER GINGERBREAD MAN.

HERE IT IS FOR YOU. BUT THIS TIME, I WILL TAKE THE MONEY.

IT WAS DONE. HEPZIBAH PYNCHEON WAS NO LADY NOW, BUT SIMPLY A FORLORN OLD MAID, KEEPER OF A SHOP. ARISTOCRACY HAD BEEN BROUGHT LOW BY A HUNGRY SCHOOL BOY!

MORE CUSTOMERS CAME IN AS THE DAY ADVANCED, OFTEN WITH LITTLE SATISFACTION TO THEMSELVES.

NO GINGER-BEER, OR ROOT-BEER? A FINE SHOP THIS IS!

MY MOTHER SAYS YOU GAVE ME THE WRONG COLOR THREAD.

A SHOP WITHOUT YEAST! WHOEVER HEARD OF SUCH A THING!

YOUR LOAF WILL NOT RISE ANY MORE THAN MINE WILL TODAY. YOU HAD BETTER SHUT UP SHOP AT ONCE!

WELL, PERHAPS I HAD.

TOWARDS NOON, HEPZIBAH SAW A PORTLY GENTLEMAN OF REMARKABLY DIGNIFIED APPEARANCE PASS ON THE OPPOSITE SIDE OF THE STREET.

WELL, COUSIN JAFFREY, YOU HAVE SEEN MY LITTLE SHOP. TAKE IT AS YOU LIKE. THIS HOUSE IS MINE, WHILE I'M ALIVE.

SHORTLY AFTERWARDS, OLD UNCLE VENNER, A HUMBLE AND FAMILIAR RESIDENT OF THE TOWN, ENTERED.

SO YOU'VE BEGUN TRADE. WELL, I'M GLAD TO SEE IT. YOUNG PEOPLE SHOULD NEVER LIVE IDLE IN THE WORLD.

I MET YOUR COUSIN, THE JUDGE, JUST NOW. HE BOWED AND SMILED AT ME.

YES, MY COUSIN JAFFREY IS THOUGHT TO HAVE A VERY PLEASANT SMILE.

IT'S TO YOUR CREDIT, MISS HEPZIBAH, TO BE WORKING, BUT IT'S NOT TO THE JUDGE'S CREDIT TO LET YOU.

IF I CHOOSE TO EARN MY BREAD, IT IS NOT JUDGE PYNCHEON'S FAULT. I WOULD RATHER DIE THAN ACCEPT THE AID HE OFFERS ME.

THEN UNCLE VENNER BECKONED HEPZIBAH NEARER TO HIM.

WHEN DO YOU EXPECT HIM HOME?

HEPZIBAH TURNED PALE AT HIS WORDS.

WHOM DO YOU MEAN?

AH? YOU DON'T LOVE TO TALK ABOUT IT. WELL, WE'LL SAY NO MORE, THOUGH THERE'S WORD OF IT ALL OVER TOWN.

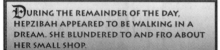

DURING THE REMAINDER OF THE DAY, HEPZIBAH APPEARED TO BE WALKING IN A DREAM. SHE BLUNDERED TO AND FRO ABOUT HER SMALL SHOP.

I ASKED FOR PINS, NOT NEEDLES!

AT LAST THE DAY ENDED. AS HEPZIBAH CLOSED THE SHOP, SHE HEARD A VEHICLE COME TO A STOP BEFORE THE HOUSE OF THE SEVEN GABLES.

AN OMNIBUS! CAN IT BE HE?

YES, A MAN WAS ALIGHTING-- BUT IT WAS ONLY TO OFFER HIS HAND TO A YOUNG GIRL, WHO NOW STOOD AT HEPZIBAH'S DOOR.

IT MUST BE LITTLE PHOEBE PYNCHEON! HOW LIKE A COUNTRY COUSIN TO COME DOWN ON A BODY THIS WAY WITHOUT SO MUCH AS A DAY'S NOTICE!

WELL, SHE CAN STAY ONE NIGHT, I SUPPOSE, BUT NO LONGER. IF CLIFFORD WERE TO FIND HER HERE, IT MIGHT DISTURB HIM.

HEPZIBAH UNBOLTED THE DOOR.

COUSIN HEPZIBAH!

COME IN, CHILD.

HEPZIBAH BADE HER YOUNG GUEST SIT DOWN.

WHY HAVE YOU COME HERE, COUSIN PHOEBE?

AS YOU KNOW, MY FATHER IS DEAD AND MY MOTHER HAS REMARRIED. IT WOULD BE DESIRABLE FOR ME TO ESTABLISH MYSELF IN ANOTHER HOME.

BUT I REALLY CAN'T SEE MY WAY CLEAR TO KEEP YOU WITH ME. I CANNOT MAKE YOUR LIFE PLEASANT, COUSIN PHOEBE, NEITHER CAN I SO MUCH AS GIVE YOU BREAD TO EAT.

I MEAN TO EARN MY OWN BREAD. AND YOU WILL FIND ME A CHEERFUL BODY.

BUT CHILD, IT IS NOT FOR ME TO SAY WHO SHALL BE A GUEST OF PYNCHEON HOUSE. ITS MASTER IS COMING.

DO YOU MEAN JUDGE PYNCHEON?

JAFFREY? HE WILL HARDLY CROSS THE THRESHOLD WHILE I LIVE! NO, YOU WILL SEE THE FACE OF HIM I SPEAK OF.

HEPZIBAH SHOWED PHOEBE THE MINIATURE SHE TREASURED.

DID YOU EVER HEAR OF YOUR COUSIN CLIFFORD PYNCHEON?

I SEEM TO HAVE HEARD SOMETHING OF HIM. BUT HAS HE NOT BEEN A LONG TIME DEAD?

PERHAPS HE HAS, CHILD. WE SHALL SEE. AND SINCE AFTER ALL I HAVE SAID YOUR COURAGE DOES NOT FAIL YOU, YOU ARE WELCOME TO SUCH A HOME AS I CAN OFFER.

PHOEBE WAS BRIGHT, CHEERFUL AND EFFICIENT. THE NEXT MORNING, WHEN THE RINGING SHOP-BELL ANNOUNCED THE FIRST CUSTOMER...

DO NOT TROUBLE YOURSELF, DEAR COUSIN. I AM SHOP-KEEPER TODAY.

HEPZIBAH WENT TO THE PASSAGE-WAY INTO THE SHOP TO NOTE HOW PHOEBE WAS MANAGING.

THIS IS LOVELY YARN.

HOW NICELY SHE DOES!

IT IS IMPOSSIBLE TO EXPLAIN HOW THE NEIGHBORHOOD BECAME AWARE OF THE GIRL'S PRESENCE, BUT SOON THERE WAS A GREAT RUN OF CUSTOM.

AS THE DAY CAME TO A CLOSE, UNCLE VENNER DROPPED IN.

WE MUST RENEW OUR STOCK, COUSIN HEPZIBAH! AND WE MUST TAKE IN SOME RAISINS, AND MOLASSES-CANDY, AND SOME APPLES, TOO.

BLESS MY EYES! WHAT A BRISK LITTLE SOUL!

THAT EVENING, IN THE GARDEN, PHOEBE MET HOLGRAVE, HER COUSIN'S LODGER.

AS YOUR COUSIN HAS DOUBTLESS MENTIONED, I AM A MAKER OF DAGUERREOTYPES. TELL ME, WHAT DO YOU THINK OF THIS SAMPLE OF MY WORK?

I KNOW THE FACE, FOR ITS STERN EYE HAS BEEN FOLLOWING ME ABOUT ALL DAY. IT IS MY PURITAN ANCESTOR, COLONEL PYNCHEON, WHOSE PORTRAIT HANGS IN THE PARLOR. BUT YOU HAVE GIVEN HIM MODERN DRESS.

I ASSURE YOU, IT IS A MODERN FACE. IT IS A SLY, HARD ONE, AS YOU CAN SEE, AND IT BELONGS TO ONE OF OUR MOST PROMINENT CITIZENS.

HE CERTAINLY LOOKS LIKE THE OLD PORTRAIT. HIS FACE IS FAR DIFFERENT FROM THE MINIATURE OF MY COUSIN CLIFFORD.

YOU HAVE SEEN THAT PICTURE? TELL ME, IS THERE ANYTHING SINISTER IN THAT FACE? COULD YOU CONCEIVE THE ORIGINAL AS BEING GUILTY OF A GREAT CRIME?

NONSENSE! THERE NEVER WAS A SWEETER FACE. IT IS ALMOST TOO GENTLE FOR A MAN'S.

THEN PHOEBE RETURNED INDOORS.

IT IS DARK IN HERE. SHALL I LIGHT A LAMP, COUSIN HEPZIBAH?

DO, IF YOU PLEASE, CHILD.

WHILE LIGHTING THE LAMP IN THE KITCHEN, PHOEBE FANCIED SHE HEARD VOICES IN THE PARLOR. WHEN SHE RETURNED...

DID YOU SPEAK TO ME JUST NOW, COUSIN HEPZIBAH?

NO, CHILD. PLEASE LEAVE THE LAMP IN THE CORNER OF THE PASSAGE-WAY. I COULD NOT BEAR THE LIGHT IN HERE.

DEAR COUSIN, IS THERE NOT SOMEONE IN THE ROOM WITH YOU?

HEPZIBAH ROSE FROM HER CHAIR.

MY DEAR LITTLE GIRL, PRAY GO TO BED. YOU WERE UP EARLY AND HAVE BEEN BUSY ALL DAY. I AM SURE YOU NEED REST. GOOD NIGHT.

GOOD NIGHT, COUSIN. IF YOU BEGIN TO LOVE ME, I AM GLAD.

THE NEXT MORNING, PHOEBE ROSE EARLY, BUT SHE FOUND HEPZIBAH ALREADY AT WORK IN THE KITCHEN

COME, CHILD, YOU MUST HELP ME. PERHAPS YOU CAN BAKE A CAKE.

WHILE THE BREAKFAST WAS BEING PREPARED, PHOEBE BROUGHT FLOWERS FROM THE GARDEN FOR THE TABLE.

THEY ARE BEAUTIFUL, CHILD. BUT DO SEE IF THE COFFEE IS DONE, OH, DEAR! OH, DEAR!

MY DEAREST COUSIN, WHAT EXCITES YOU SO?

HUSH! HUSH! HE IS COMING!

LET HIM SEE YOU FIRST, PHOEBE. HE ALWAYS LIKED BRIGHT FACES. MINE IS OLD NOW, AND THERE ARE TEARS IN MY EYES. HE NEVER COULD ABIDE TEARS.

THEN HEPZIBAH RUSHED FORWARD AND THREW OPEN THE DOOR.

LATER, THEY MOVED TO THE PARLOR.

HEPZIBAH! WHY DO YOU KEEP THAT ODIOUS PICTURE? TAKE IT DOWN AT ONCE! I CANNOT BEAR IT!

DEAR CLIFFORD, YOU KNOW THAT CANNOT BE.

SUDDENLY THE RING OF THE SHOP-BELL SOUNDED THROUGHOUT THE HOUSE.

GOOD HEAVENS! WHAT A HATEFUL CLAMOR! WHAT CAN IT BE?

DEAR CLIFFORD, THAT UGLY NOISE— PRAY, RUN, PHOEBE, AND SEE WHO IS THERE—IS OUR SHOP-BELL. FOR YOU MUST KNOW, WE ARE VERY POOR.

DO YOU THINK, CLIFFORD, I HAVE BROUGHT DISGRACE ON THIS HOUSE BY OPENING A LITTLE SHOP? ARE YOU ASHAMED OF ME?

DISGRACE? SHAME? DO YOU SPEAK THOSE WORDS TO ME? WHAT GREATER SHAME CAN BEFALL ME BEYOND WHAT I HAVE ALREADY ENDURED?

WHEN PHOEBE GOT TO THE SHOP, SHE BEHELD THE LITTLE DEVOURER OF GINGERBREAD MEN.

FOLKS SAY OLD MAID PYNCHEON'S BROTHER HAS GOT HOME.

SO CLIFFORD IS HER BROTHER! I DIDN'T KNOW THAT!

AS THE BOY LEFT, A GENTLEMAN ENTERED.

UNLESS I AM MISTAKEN, YOU ARE PHOEBE, MY OWN LITTLE KINSWOMAN. I AM JUDGE PYNCHEON. SURELY YOU HAVE HEARD OF ME.

THE JUDGE BENT DOWN TO DELIVER A COUSINLY KISS. BUT FROM SOME INSTINCT, PHOEBE STEPPED QUICKLY BACK, LEAVING THE GENTLEMAN RATHER ABSURDLY KISSING THE EMPTY AIR.

AN UGLY LOOK SWEPT ACROSS THE JUDGE'S FACE.

I LIKE THAT, COUSIN PHOEBE. A PRETTY GIRL CAN NEVER BE TOO CAREFUL OF HER LIPS.

ALL AT ONCE, IT STRUCK PHOEBE THAT HERE WAS THE ORIGINAL OF THE MINIATURE WHICH HOLGRAVE HAD SHOWN HER. AND—STRANGE FANTASY—IT SEEMED THAT THE VERY FOUNDER OF THE HOUSE OF THE SEVEN GABLES HAD NOW STEPPED INTO THE SHOP.

PHOEBE WAS FAR TOO SENSIBLE TO ENTERTAIN THIS FANTASTIC IDEA FOR LONG. STILL, WHEN THE JUDGE HAPPENED TO CLEAR HIS THROAT, SHE ALMOST THOUGHT SHE HEARD THE VOICE OF MATTHEW MAULE SAYING, "'GOD WILL GIVE HIM BLOOD TO DRINK.'"

OH!

WHAT IS THE MATTER WITH YOU, YOUNG WOMAN? AH, BUT NO WONDER YOU ARE UPSET. HEPZIBAH'S GUEST MIGHT WELL STARTLE AN INNOCENT YOUNG GIRL.

THERE IS NO FRIGHTFUL GUEST, BUT ONLY A GENTLE, CHILDLIKE MAN, WHOM I BELIEVE TO BE MY COUSIN'S BROTHER.

I REJOICE TO HEAR SO FAVORABLE A REPORT OF CLIFFORD. MANY YEARS AGO, I HAD GREAT AFFECTION FOR HIM. HEAVEN GRANT HE HAS REPENTED OF HIS PAST SINS.

NOBODY, I FANCY, COULD HAVE FEWER TO REPENT OF.

IS IT POSSIBLE THAT YOU KNOW NOTHING OF CLIFFORD PYNCHEON'S HISTORY? WELL, NO MATTER. IS CLIFFORD IN THE PARLOR? I WILL JUST STEP IN AND SEE.

As the days passed, Phoebe became essential to the comfort of her two forlorn companions.

THANK YOU, LITTLE PHOEBE, FOR THESE LOVELY FLOWERS.

The grime and sordidness of the house of the seven gables seemed to vanish at her appearance.

WHAT A NICE LITTLE HOUSEWIFE YOU ARE!

Every Sunday afternoon, there was a sober little festival in the garden, in which Holgrave and Uncle Venner always joined.

I REALLY ENJOY THESE QUIET LITTLE MEETINGS. THIS IS THE WAY THINGS SHOULD BE—PEACEFUL AND HAPPY.

But Clifford was not without moments of sudden sadness.

'TIS LATE! IT IS LATE! I WANT MY HAPPINESS!

ONE SUNDAY MORNING, AFTER PHOEBE HAD GONE TO CHURCH.

I THINK THAT IF I WERE IN CHURCH, I COULD PRAY AGAIN, WHEN SO MANY HUMAN SOULS WERE PRAYING ALL AROUND ME.

DEAR BROTHER, LET US GO!

THEY MADE THEMSELVES READY, AS BEST THEY COULD, IN THEIR OLD-FASHIONED GARMENTS. BUT AS THEY OPENED THE DOOR...

WE CANNOT GO, HEPZIBAH! IT WOULD NOT BE FITTING. I CANNOT BEAR THAT I SHOULD BE FRIGHTFUL TO MY FELLOW BEINGS, AND THAT CHILDREN SHOULD CLING TO THEIR MOTHERS AT THE SIGHT OF ME.

WE ARE GHOSTS, HEPZIBAH. WE HAVE NO RIGHT AMONG HUMAN BEINGS—NO RIGHT ANYWHERE BUT IN THIS OLD HOUSE, WHICH HAS A CURSE ON IT, AND WHICH, THEREFORE, WE ARE DOOMED TO HAUNT.

WE CANNOT FLEE. OUR JAILER HAS LEFT OUR DOOR AJAR IN MOCKERY.

ON ANOTHER OCCASION, CLIFFORD, IN A CHILDLIKE STATE, SAT BY AN OPEN WINDOW AMUSING HIMSELF WITH A CHILD'S PASTIME.

JUST AS JUDGE PYNCHEON HAPPENED TO BE PASSING, A LARGE BUBBLE SAILED MAJESTICALLY DOWN AND BURST AGAINST HIS NOSE.

AHA, COUSIN CLIFFORD! WHAT? STILL BLOWING SOAP BUBBLES?

THE JUDGE'S SMILE HAD BEEN PLEASANT, BUT CLIFFORD SHRANK BACK IN FEAR AND DREAD.

LET JAFFREY SMILE AS HE WILL. BUT PUT HIM IN A SKULL CAP AND A BLACK CLOAK AND NO ONE COULD DOUBT BUT THAT OLD COLONEL PYNCHEON HAD COME ALIVE AGAIN.

SOME DAYS LATER, PHOEBE AND HOLGRAVE MET IN THE GARDEN. THEY SPOKE OF CLIFFORD.

HE SEEMS HAPPY AS A CHILD. BUT, LIKE A CHILD, HE IS VERY EASILY DISTURBED.

HOW I SHOULD LIKE TO HAVE YOUR OPPORTUNITY TO OBSERVE CLIFFORD!

HOW STRANGE THAT YOU SHOULD WISH IT! WHAT IS COUSIN CLIFFORD TO YOU?

NOTHING, OF COURSE. BUT I HAVE AN INTEREST IN THE PAST – AND HOW IT WEIGHS UPON THE PRESENT LIKE A GIANT'S DEAD BODY.

SHALL WE NEVER BE RID OF THE PAST? WE READ DEAD MEN'S BOOKS, WE BELIEVE WHAT DEAD MEN TELL US. WE EVEN LIVE IN DEAD MEN'S HOUSES, AS IN THIS HOUSE OF THE SEVEN GABLES!

THEN WHY DO YOU LIVE HERE?

I DWELL HERE THAT I MAY LEARN BETTER TO HATE THE PAST IT EXPRESSES SO WELL – THE ODIOUS PAST, WITH ALL ITS BAD INFLUENCE ON THE PRESENT.

DID YOU EVER HEAR THE STORY OF MATTHEW MAULE, AND THE CURSE HE PLACED UPON YOUR ANCESTOR, COLONEL PYNCHEON?

YES, INDEED. COUSIN HEPZIBAH SEEMS TO THINK ALL THE CALAMITIES OF THE PYNCHEONS BEGAN WITH THAT CURSE.

AND YOU, MR. HOLGRAVE, LOOK AS THOUGH YOU THINK SO, TOO.

I DO THINK SO, AND NOT AS A SUPERSTITION, BUT AS SOMETHING PROVED BY UNQUESTIONABLE FACT.

UNDER THOSE SEVEN GABLES, THERE HAVE BEEN, SINCE THE COLONEL'S TIME, NOTHING BUT MISERY, DEATH AND DISGRACE.

THEN AGAIN I ASK, WHY DO YOU STAY HERE?

IT IS INTERESTING TO OBSERVE THIS DRAMA, WHICH FOR THESE MANY YEARS HAS BEEN PLAYED ON THE VERY GROUND WHERE NOW WE TREAD, AND I HAVE THE CONVICTION THAT THE END OF THE DRAMA IS NEAR.

BUT THE PLAY COSTS THE PERFORMERS TOO MUCH AND YOU, THE AUDIENCE, ARE TOO COLD-HEARTED.

FORGIVE ME, PHOEBE. LET US PART FRIENDS, FOR I HEAR YOU LEAVE SOON ON A VISIT HOME.

I WILL ONLY BE GONE A FEW DAYS. GOODBYE. I DID NOT MEAN TO BE ANGRY.

AFTER PHOEBE'S DEPARTURE, A STORM SET IN, MAKING THE OLD HOUSE MORE CHEERLESS THAN EVER.

I HAVE NOT THE STRENGTH TO LEAVE MY BED. THE WARM SUNSHINE HAS GONE WITH PHOEBE.

ON THE FIFTH DAY OF THE STORM, THE SHOP-BELL RANG, AND JUDGE PYNCHEON ENTERED.

I HAVE COME TO SEE HOW THIS TERRIBLE WEATHER AFFECTS OUR POOR CLIFFORD. I WOULD LIKE TO SEE HIM.

YOU CANNOT SEE HIM. CLIFFORD HAS KEPT TO HIS BED SINCE YESTERDAY.

WHAT! IS HE ILL? THEN I MUST AND I WILL SEE HIM! WHAT IF HE SHOULD DIE?

HE WILL NOT DIE – UNLESS HE IS HOUNDED TO DEATH BY YOU, WHO LONG AGO ATTEMPTED IT.

YOU ARE UNJUST. I DID NOTHING AT CLIFFORD'S TRIAL BUT GIVE TESTIMONY REQUIRED BY LAW. NO ONE HAS SHED MORE TEARS FOR HIS CALAMITY THAN I.

IN GOD'S NAME, STOP THIS LOATHSOME PRETENSE OF AFFECTION. YOU HATE HIM! SAY SO, LIKE A MAN!

JUDGE PYNCHEON'S FACE TURNED HARD AND COLD.

COUSIN HEPZIBAH, IT IS MY PURPOSE TO SEE CLIFFORD BEFORE I LEAVE THIS HOUSE.

ARE YOU SO BLIND YOU DO NOT SEE IT WAS MY INFLUENCE THAT SET CLIFFORD FREE FROM PRISON?

YOU? I WILL NEVER BELIEVE IT! HE OWED HIS IMPRISONMENT TO YOU; HIS RELEASE WAS GOD'S WILL.

I HAD CLIFFORD SET FREE, FOR A PURPOSE OF MY OWN. AND FOR THIS PURPOSE, I MUST SEE HIM—NOW.

I AM CONVINCED THAT ONLY A PORTION OF OUR UNCLE'S WEALTH, WHICH WAS BEQUEATHED TO ME UPON HIS DEATH, HAS EVER BEEN FOUND. I BELIEVE YOUR BROTHER CAN GIVE ME A CLUE TO THE REMAINDER.

CLIFFORD KNOW OF HIDDEN WEALTH? IMPOSSIBLE!

I AM CERTAIN OF THIS. HE TOLD ME SO HIMSELF!

WHEN WE WERE CHILDREN, CLIFFORD BOASTED OF HAVING THE SECRET OF OUR UNCLE'S GREAT WEALTH. I BELIEVE IF HE CHOOSES—AND CHOOSE HE MUST—HE CAN TELL ME WHERE TO FIND EVIDENCE OF OUR UNCLE'S MISSING PROPERTY.

AND WHAT IF HE REFUSES? WHAT IF HE HAS NO SUCH KNOWLEDGE?

THE WHOLE TOWN KNOWS OF HIS ODD BEHAVIOR. I, MYSELF, CAN TESTIFY TO HIS CHILDLIKE PASTIMES.

IF CLIFFORD SHALL REFUSE ME, I SHALL RECOMMEND HE BE CONFINED TO A MENTAL ASYLUM FOR THE REMAINDER OF HIS LIFE.

YOU CANNOT MEAN IT! IT IS YOU THAT ARE DISEASED IN MIND, NOT CLIFFORD!

TALK SENSE, HEPZIBAH. I HAVE TOLD YOU MY DETERMINATION.

YOU ARE STRONGER THAN I. I WILL CALL CLIFFORD. BUT BE MERCIFUL TO HIM—FOR GOD IS LOOKING AT YOU, JAFFREY PYNCHEON!

THE JUDGE FOLLOWED HIS COUSIN FROM THE SHOP INTO THE PARLOR, AND FLUNG HIMSELF INTO COLONEL PYNCHEON'S CHAIR.

BID CLIFFORD COME QUICKLY. I HAVE IMPORTANT AFFAIRS TO ATTEND TO THIS DAY.

HEPZIBAH WENT TO CLIFFORD'S DOOR AND KNOCKED.

CLIFFORD! MAY I COME IN?

THERE WAS NO ANSWER. HEPZIBAH KNOCKED AGAIN AND AGAIN. THEN SHE OPENED THE DOOR.

CLIFFORD, WHERE ARE YOU?

CLIFFORD WAS NOWHERE TO BE FOUND. HEPZIBAH, TERRIFIED AT WHAT MIGHT HAVE HAPPENED TO HIM, HASTENED BACK TO THE PARLOR.

CLIFFORD HAS GONE! HELP, JAFFREY! YOU MUST HELP ME SEEK HIM!

THERE WAS NO ANSWER.

DO YOU HEAR ME? CLIFFORD IS GONE!

AT THAT MOMENT...

CLIFFORD!

WE CAN LAUGH NOW, SING, PLAY, DO WHAT WE WILL! THE WEIGHT IS GONE, HEPZIBAH!

HEPZIBAH WENT INTO THE PARLOR, BUT ALMOST IMMEDIATELY RETURNED.

MY GOD! WHAT IS TO BECOME OF US?

COME! WE STAY HERE TOO LONG. LET US LEAVE THE HOUSE TO OUR COUSIN JAFFREY. HE WILL TAKE GOOD CARE OF IT.

THEY PUT ON THEIR CLOAKS AND DEPARTED.

AND JUDGE PYNCHEON WAS LEFT SITTING IN THE HOME OF HIS FOREFATHERS, ALL BY HIMSELF.

HEPZIBAH AND CLIFFORD MET FEW PEOPLE AS THEY PASSED TO THE CENTER OF THE TOWN.

THE PITILESS EAST WIND SET HEPZIBAH'S TEETH CHATTERING IN HER HEAD. HER MIND SEEMED TO BE ADRIFT.

CLIFFORD! CLIFFORD! IS THIS NOT A DREAM?

A DREAM, HEPZIBAH? ON THE CONTRARY, I HAVE NEVER BEEN AWAKE BEFORE.

BY PURPOSE OR BY CHANCE, CLIFFORD LED HER TO THE RAILWAY STATION. THEY BOARDED A TRAIN, AND WERE SWEPT AWAY.

BUT WHEN THE TRAIN REACHED ANOTHER STATION, THEY LEFT THEIR CAR. CLIFFORD'S WILD MOOD HAD VANISHED.

YOU MUST TAKE THE LEAD NOW. DO WITH ME AS YOU WILL.

O GOD, OUR FATHER, ARE WE NOT THY CHILDREN? HAVE MERCY UPON US!

MEANWHILE, JUDGE PYNCHEON STILL LINGERED IN THE PARLOR OF THE HOUSE OF THE SEVEN GABLES. HE HAD NOT STIRRED HAND OR FOOT SINCE HIS TWO RELATIVES FLED.

THERE IS A LEGEND THAT, AT MIDNIGHT, ALL DEAD PYNCHEONS ASSEMBLE IN THE PARLOR UNDER THE SEVEN GABLES, TO SEE IF THE PORTRAIT OF THEIR ANCESTOR STILL KEEPS ITS PLACE ON THE WALL.

THE PYNCHEON WHO NOW SITS BENEATH THAT PORTRAIT BELIEVES IN NO SUCH NONSENSE. SUCH, AT LEAST, WAS HIS CREED A FEW HOURS AGO.

AND YET—PERHAPS IT IS ONLY THE QUIVER OF MOONBEAMS—BUT IS IT NOT A FIGURE IN A PURITAN'S BLACK COAT WHO NOW PLACES HIS HAND UPON THE FRAME? AND THOSE OTHERS...?

ALL TRY THE PICTURE-FRAME. WHAT DO THESE GHOSTLY PEOPLE SEEK? SOMETHING ABOUT THE PICTURE PERPLEXES THESE POOR PYNCHEONS.

CAN WE BELIEVE OUR EYES? NOW THE JUDGE ENTERS. BUT NOW CAN IT BE THE JUDGE WHEN HE IS STILL SEATED IN THE ANCESTRAL CHAIR? YET HE, TOO, TRIES TO PEEP BEHIND THE FRAME.

AND IN A CORNER, MEANWHILE, STANDS A MAN WITH A CARPENTER'S RULE, WHO JEERS AND LAUGHS.

ABSURD LEGEND! WHO CAN BELIEVE IN GHOST TALES IN THESE MODERN DAYS? IT WILL SOON BE MORNING. THEN WE WILL BREATHE MORE FREELY, AND RETURN TO OUR STORY.

UNCLE VENNER WAS THE FIRST PERSON STIRRING IN THE NEIGHBORHOOD THE NEXT MORNING. HE SAW HOLGRAVE AT HIS WINDOW.

WELL, AND DID THE WIND KEEP YOU AWAKE LAST NIGHT?

IT DID, INDEED! IF I BELIEVED IN GHOSTS, I SHOULD HAVE THOUGHT ALL THE OLD PYNCHEONS WERE RUNNING RIOT IN THE LOWER ROOMS. BUT IT IS VERY QUIET THERE NOW.

LATER IN THE DAY, PHOEBE RETURNED TO THE HOUSE OF THE SEVEN GABLES.

THAT IS STRANGE. THE SHOP-DOOR IS LOCKED.

SHE WENT INTO THE GARDEN.

SOMETHING IS AMISS. NO ONE HAS BEEN HERE FOR DAYS.

SHE TRIED THE GARDEN DOOR, BUT IT WAS ALSO LOCKED. SHE KNOCKED, HOWEVER, AND THE DOOR WAS DRAWN OPEN.

SHE STEPPED ACROSS THE THRESHOLD. IMMEDIATELY, THE DOOR CLOSED BEHIND HER, AND A HAND GRASPED HER OWN.

MR. HOLGRAVE! WHY IS THE HOUSE SO DESERTED? WHERE ARE HEPZIBAH AND CLIFFORD?

GONE!

A TERRIBLE EVENT HAS HAPPENED, BUT NOT TO THEM. NOR DO I BELIEVE IT WAS ANY FAULT OF THEIRS.

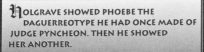

HOLGRAVE SHOWED PHOEBE THE DAGUERREOTYPE HE HAD ONCE MADE OF JUDGE PYNCHEON. THEN HE SHOWED HER ANOTHER.

YOU SAW THIS FIRST LIKENESS SOME WEEKS AGO, IN THE GARDEN. HERE IS ANOTHER OF THE SAME SUBJECT, TAKEN WITHIN THIS HALF HOUR.

THIS IS DEATH! JUDGE PYNCHEON IS DEAD!

THE JUDGE IS DEAD, AND IN THAT STATE, HE SITS IN THE NEXT ROOM. HEPZIBAH AND CLIFFORD HAVE VANISHED.

THEIR FLIGHT THROWS THE WORST POSSIBLE COLORING OVER THIS EVENT. YET I AM SURE THE JUDGE DID NOT COME UNFAIRLY TO HIS END. THIS MODE OF DEATH HAS BEEN COMMON TO THE PYNCHEONS FOR GENERATIONS.

"MATTHEW MAULE'S PROPHECY ABOUT COLONEL PYNCHEON WAS PROBABLY FOUNDED ON A KNOWLEDGE OF THIS TENDENCY.

GOD WILL GIVE HIM BLOOD TO DRINK!

"I AM CONVINCED THAT THE UNCLE WHOM CLIFFORD WAS ACCUSED OF MURDERING DIED IN THE SAME MANNER AS COLONEL PYNCHEON, BUT JUDGE PYNCHEON ARRANGED THE EVIDENCE TO MAKE CLIFFORD SEEM GUILTY OF THE OLD MAN'S DEATH."

NOW THE JUDGE'S OWN DEATH, IN THE SAME SUDDEN WAY, IS A PUNISHMENT FOR HIS WICKEDNESS, AND MAKES PLAIN CLIFFORD'S INNOCENCE.

THEN...

THE MAN WHO LIES DEAD YONDER WAS A SHADOW ON MY LIFE. BUT WHEN YOU CROSSED THE THRESHOLD, JOY DROVE AWAY THAT SHADOW.

IT SEEMS A SIN TO THINK OF JOY AT SUCH A TIME.

THIS BLACK MOMENT HAS BECOME A BLESSED ONE. IT MUST NOT PASS WITHOUT THE SPOKEN WORD. I LOVE YOU.

HOW CAN YOU LOVE A SIMPLE GIRL LIKE ME?

YOU ARE MY ONLY POSSIBILITY OF HAPPINESS. DO YOU LOVE ME, PHOEBE?

LOOK INTO MY HEART. YOU KNOW I LOVE YOU.

BUT SOON THE EARTH-DREAM WAS DISTURBED.

HARK! SOMEBODY IS AT THE STREET-DOOR.

THEY HEARD FOOTSTEPS IN THE HALLWAY.

CAN IT BE?

THEN THEY HEARD THE VOICES.

WE RETURN TO A DREARY HOME. BUT YOU DID WELL TO BRING ME BACK, HEPZIBAH.

BUT THE HOUSE WAS NOT AS DREARY AS CLIFFORD THOUGHT. THE NEXT MOMENT...

IT IS OUR OWN LITTLE PHOEBE! AND HOLGRAVE!

THANK GOD, YOU ARE BACK!

WHEN CLIFFORD SAW HOLGRAVE AND PHOEBE TOGETHER, HIS KEEN AND DELICATE INSIGHT TOLD HIM WHAT HAD PASSED BETWEEN THEM.

I THOUGHT OF YOU BOTH AS I PASSED THE FLOWERS BLOOMING IN FRONT OF THE HOUSE. AND SO THE FLOWER OF LOVE HAS LIKEWISE BLOOMED IN THIS OLD HOUSE TODAY.

MEDICAL AUTHORITIES PROVED THE SUDDEN DEATH OF JUDGE PYNCHEON WAS A NATURAL ONE. THEN PEOPLE BEGAN TO THINK ABOUT THE DEATH OF HIS UNCLE, THIRTY YEARS BEFORE.

A THEORY AROSE THAT ONE NIGHT, YOUNG JAFFREY PYNCHEON WAS SEARCHING HIS UNCLE'S PRIVATE DRAWERS, WHEN HE WAS SURPRISED BY THE OLD MAN.

IN THE HORROR AND SHOCK OF THE DISCOVERY, THE UNCLE SEEMED TO CHOKE WITH BLOOD. HE FELL UPON THE FLOOR, STRIKING HIS HEAD ON A TABLE.

HE'S DEAD! WHAT SHALL I DO?

I KNOW! I WILL AVERT SUSPICION FROM MYSELF AND TURN IT TOWARDS COUSIN CLIFFORD.

THUS CLIFFORD WAS FOUND GUILTY OF HIS UNCLE'S DEATH. NOW, THIRTY YEARS LATER, CLIFFORD'S INNOCENCE WAS ESTABLISHED AND WITH THE JUDGE'S DEATH, CLIFFORD, HEPZIBAH AND PHOEBE INHERITED HIS FORTUNE.

WE SHALL LEAVE THIS DISMAL HOUSE AND MOVE TO COUSIN JAFFREY'S COUNTRY HOME.

ON THE DAY SET FOR THEIR DEPARTURE, THE PYNCHEONS ASSEMBLED IN THE PARLOR, WITH HOLGRAVE AND UNCLE VENNER.

THAT PICTURE! I SEEM TO RECALL HAVING ONCE FANCIED IT HELD A SECRET FOR ME. BUT I DON'T REMEMBER WHAT IT WAS.

PERHAPS I CAN HELP YOU. IT IS UNLIKELY THAT ANYONE UNACQUAINTED WITH THE SECRET WOULD EVER TOUCH THIS SPRING.

THE SPRING WAS SO EATEN THROUGH WITH RUST THAT THE PORTRAIT FELL TO THE FLOOR.

YES! THE SECRET SPRING! I REMEMBER IT NOW! I DISCOVERED IT LONG AGO, AS A CHILD.

IN THE RECESS IN THE WALL LAY A FOLDED SHEET OF PARCHMENT.

HOLGRAVE UNFOLDED IT.

THIS IS THE DEED TO THE EASTERN LANDS WHICH ALL THE HEIRS OF COLONEL PYNCHEON SOUGHT IN VAIN. THE LAND, OF COURSE, HAS LONG SINCE BEEN SETTLED. THE DEED IS NOW WORTHLESS.

SO THAT IS THE SECRET WEALTH JAFFREY THOUGHT CLIFFORD KNEW OF! CLIFFORD PROBABLY MADE A FAIRY TALE OUT OF HIS DISCOVERY, AND JAFFREY THOUGHT IT WAS REAL.

BUT HOW CAME YOU TO KNOW THE SECRET OF THE PORTRAIT?

MY DEAREST PHOEBE, HOW WILL IT PLEASE YOU TO ASSUME THE NAME OF MAULE? FOR I AM A DESCENDANT OF OLD MATTHEW.

YOU ARE A MAULE?

YES. IN THIS LONG DRAMA OF RIGHT AND WRONG, I REPRESENT THE OLD WIZARD.

THE SECRET OF THE PORTRAIT IS THE ONLY INHERITANCE THAT HAS COME DOWN TO ME FROM MY ANCESTORS.

"THOMAS MAULE, THE SON OF THE EXECUTED MATTHEW, WHILE BUILDING THIS HOUSE CONSTRUCTED THE RECESS TO HIDE AWAY THE INDIAN DEED, TO WHICH HE HAD SOMEHOW GAINED ACCESS."

THUS THE PYNCHEONS LOST THEIR VAST EASTERN LANDS BECAUSE THEY WANTED MATTHEW MAULE'S LITTLE GARDEN-GROUND.

THEN, AS THEY PREPARED TO LEAVE.

AND SO EVERYONE—WITH THE EXCEPTION OF UNCLE VENNER, WHO WAS TO FOLLOW LATER—SET OUT FOR THEIR NEW HOME. AS HEPZIBAH WAS ABOUT TO STEP INTO THE CARRIAGE.

UNCLE VENNER, THERE IS A COTTAGE IN OUR NEW GARDEN. WE ARE GOING TO FURNISH IT JUST FOR YOU.

WELL, BLESS MY SOUL. YOU HAVE MADE ME THE HAPPIEST MAN ALIVE.

HERE, MY LAD, IS ENOUGH SILVER TO FILL EVEN YOUR VAST INTERIOR WITH GINGERBREAD.

AND SO HEPZIBAH AND CLIFFORD AND PHOEBE BADE A FINAL FAREWELL TO THE ABODE OF THEIR FOREFATHERS. OLD MATTHEW MAULE HAD, AT LAST, WITHDRAWN HIS CURSE. PERHAPS HE HAD NOW CAST A SPELL OF LOVE UPON THE FORMER DWELLERS OF THE HOUSE OF THE SEVEN GABLES.

THE END

THE HOUSE OF THE SEVEN GABLES
NATHANIEL HAWTHORNE

Are the sins of one generation inherited by the next? Can you be punished for an act of your ancestor's? Could your failures be the evidence of wrongdoing of your great-grandfather's, or grandmother's?

These are probably not the first questions that leap to our minds in the face of a crisis, but we do look to history for solutions to our own dilemmas. Although Nathaniel Hawthorne set his "romance," *The House of the Seven Gables*, in the mid-nineteenth century New England of his day, the events refer back to an earlier era. Secret knowledge from the past allows certain characters to make sense of what they see. Others, those who have forgotten (or never knew) the history, simply can't understand the actions that take place in front of their very eyes.

Hawthorne's novel is equal parts romance, ghost story, history, and myth. Upon its publication in April of 1851, *The House of the Seven Gables* met with remarkable success. American readers were fascinated by the legacy of witchcraft and sorcery in their midst, and the promise of new and magical technologies. Since Hawthorne's time, many writers have picked up on his themes of greed and lost youth, unjust punishments, and personal redemption. Following Hawthorne, each generation of writers seems to find a new perspective on the Salem witch trials and a new relevance to their own time. Even as the 20th-century fades into the 21st, Hawthorne's ghosts continue to creep quietly across the American landscape.

The Author

Appropriately enough for a writer who has been at the center of American literature and national culture for a century and a half, Hawthorne was born on July 4, 1804. The author (who was born with the name Hathorne) was born in Salem, Massachusetts, and his parents' ancestry stretched back through a number of well-known New England families. Hawthorne's own heritage—cultural, regional, and financial—shows up in his writings continually.

Hawthorne's childhood has been difficult for researchers to reconstruct, but a few central facts about his early years have been established. From the beginning of his life, Nathaniel's father was absent, sailing far away as a captain in the East Indian Marine Society. In 1808, his father died of yellow fever in New Guinea. Soon after, Mrs. Hathorne moved herself and her three young children to live with her family, the Mannings.

From contemporary accounts, Nathaniel was always a quiet, sensitive, imaginative youth who spent much of his time alone. Later in life, he referred to his father as a person who similarly tended toward seclusion. On the other hand, the Manning household was a lively one, with at least 10 family members all together, plus the three

Hathornes. Nathaniel's sister Elizabeth called their childhood home busy as a "tavern" and suggested that their aunts and uncles were entirely welcoming to Nathaniel and his two sisters.

Indeed, the most unpleasant aspect of the author's childhood was that—even for an early-nine-teenth century family—members of Hawthorne's family seemed to die with surprising regularity. In addition to losing their father, the Hathorne children witnessed cousins, grandparents, aunts and uncles die in the space of only a few years. In fact, one year (1813) Nathaniel saw four members of his extended family die, some at young ages. Perhaps unsurprisingly, sudden deaths (especially those occurring within the same family) play a significant role in the plot of *The House of the Seven Gables*.

Although most young men from middle- to upper-class families in Salem sent their sons to Harvard College, Hawthorne went to the less expensive Bowdoin College in Maine. With the support of friends in college, he decided to become a writer, but many years passed before he fulfilled this goal. He returned to Salem in 1825, after completing his studies at Bowdoin, without clear prospects of employment. He published his first novel privately in 1828 and a number of stories in local newspapers and magazines over the following years.

Hawthorne's professional break-through came in 1837 when he published his *Twice-told Tales* with his name boldly blazoned on the title page (his previous publications had been anonymous). Two years later he married Sophia Peabody and moved to Concord, Massachusetts.

Meanwhile, he wrote children's books and re-edited his *Tales*. Working first as a measurer and then a surveyor, Hawthorne continued to write, publishing another collection of stories in 1846. In 1850, he published his novel, *The Scarlet Letter,* and the following year *The House of the Seven Gables*, making him one of the most prominent authors in the country. Hawthorne continued to publish stories and novels until his death in 1864, but his best-known work remains that which he accomplished in the 40s and 50s.

The remarkable aspect of *The House of the Seven Gables* is that no char-acter clearly functions as the pro-tagonist or hero. At different points in the novel, different char-acters seem to become the central figure, but none of them hold the attention of the narrator through the end of the work. We cannot know why Hawthorne organizes the novel in this way, but we can recognize the fact that the author was clearly fascinated with a number of his characters and wanted to bring as many of them as possible to the fore.

Colonel Pyncheon begins the sequence of events that sets the story in motion. A seventeenth-century forebear of the Pyncheon family, the Colonel is a man of clear purpose and unwavering will. He claims that a tract of land occu-pied by another man (Matthew Maule) should rightfully be his. Hawthorne goes to great lengths to emphasize that this story is currently known only from "tradition" and rumor, and therefore can't be fully trusted. Still, the outline of events seems clear: using the connections he has as a rich and powerful man in his community, Pyncheon makes his dispute over the land a public battle.

This dispute occurs at the time of the Salem witchcraft panic of 1692, and Pyncheon plays a major role in the prosecution of suspected sorcerers. Unsurprisingly, he singles out Maule, and Maule is condemned as a wizard. After Maule's execution, Pyncheon takes over his land and immediately builds a mansion, the house in which his family will dwell for generations. Pyncheon's neighbors are aware of what lay behind the Colonel's accusation of Matthew Maule and—although they don't doubt his sincerity as a hunter of witches—they are surprised that Pyncheon would choose to live on the grounds that he acquired under such circumstances. **In an important irony, the new owner of the land hires the most capable carpenter in the town, unconcerned**

BUT THE OLD PURITAN WAS NOT A MAN TO BE TURNED ASIDE BY A CORPSE. HE EVEN HIRED, AS HEAD CARPENTER, THE SON OF THE MAN FROM WHOSE GRIP THE SOIL HAD BEEN WRESTED.

'TIS STRANGE HOW TOM MAULE SERVES HIS FATHER'S DEADLY ENEMY.

that the man he hires is also the son of the man he had executed, Matthew Maule Pyncheon's moral deafness and his inflexible sense of purpose lead him to hire Thomas Maule as the architect of

the House of the Seven Gables. After the mansion has been completed, Pyncheon's neighbors find him dead. No doctor can find any certain cause of death and so the coroners pronounce him the victim of "Sudden Death." The townspeople, however, prefer to recall the curse that Matthew Maule put on Pyncheon in the moments before his execution.

Matthew Maule is a character of Hawthorne's invention, but he's based on an actual person. Thomas Maule (the name that the author gives Matthew's son) lived from 1645 until 1724 as a Quaker in the New England town of Salem. *Thomas Maule was persecuted, not for witchcraft, but for practicing a different religion from that of the majority of the town.* He wrote a

AND IN A CORNER, MEANWHILE, STANDS A MAN WITH A CARPENTER'S RULE, WHO JEERS AND LAUGHS.

book a few years after the Salem witchcraft panic had subsided (1695), in which he roundly criticizes the proceedings. Thomas Maule was imprisoned for writing the book, but (unlike Matthew Maule) he was not executed.

Hawthorne's Matthew Maule is an outsider who suffers because he's powerless to prevent Colonel Pyncheon from indicting him. The author neither confirms or denies Maule's supernatural powers. Although Hawthorne refers repeatedly (in the book and in letters and notebooks) to the entire event of the Salem trials as one in which the community was "miserably deceived," he also preserves Maule's mysterious and possibly magical character. With the executioner's noose around his neck, Matthew Maule utters his bitter "prophecy" with "a ghastly look" at Pyncheon: "God will give him blood to drink." Regardless of cause, the curse sticks to the family, and generations of Pyncheon men die mysterious and solitary deaths.

AH, MR. HOLGRAVE, I NEVER CAN GO THROUGH WITH IT! I AM TOO OLD, TOO FEEBLE! AND TO THINK THAT A BORN LADY SHOULD BE REDUCED TO RUNNING A SHOP!

Passing down the House of the Seven Gables as a sign of family continuity and permanence, the Pyncheons also bequeath the curse that goes along with the property: One of Hawthorne's central preoccupations in this book is whether each generation (knowing that they received the house as a result of injustice) is as worthy of punishment as the original swindler. The author calls this question the "awful query" that drives his narrative:

…whether each inheritor of the property—conscious of wrong, and failing to rectify it—did not commit anew the great guilt of his ancestor, and incur all its original responsibilities. And supposing this to be the case, would it not be a far truer mode of expression to say, of the Pyncheon family, that they inherited a great misfortune, than the reverse?

Hepzibah Pyncheon is the occupant of the House of the Seven Gables at the present time of the narrative. She is a cousin of the previous resident and survives only under conditions of poverty and solitude. Hepzibah, though an ultimately sympathetic character, is distinguished largely by her unfriendly demeanor and lack of contact with her neighbors. She fantasizes that an unknown relative will rescue her from her financial ruin, but in order to ensure her short-term survival, she opens a cent shop (a kind of low-end general store) at the side of the house. The comedy in this act (the author calls it "overpoweringly ridiculous") stems from the fact that none of the townspeople know or enjoy Hepzibah's company so they certainly wouldn't seek it out by shopping at her store.

Hepzibah spends much of her time lamenting the fact that her noble birth and aristocratic background haven't shielded her from financial woes. **Her cent shop represents (to her) the end of her status as a member of the upper class** When she calls herself "a lady," Hepzibah refers both to her class *and* her gender; she means that, as the child of the upper classes, she shouldn't have to work for a living, but also that, as a woman, she should not even consider a profession. When Holgrave tries to comfort her, she replies that he, as "a man—a young man," has "a view to seeking your fortune. But I was born a lady." Holgrave, thinking of her

What Is A Daguerreotype?

Holgrave's profession isn't absolutely crucial to the plot of *The House of the Seven Gables*, but it is an important aspect of the mid-nineteenth century world that Hawthorne evokes. "The artist," as the narrator repeatedly calls Holgrave, voices ideas that aren't far from the author's own. Hawthorne certainly did not choose the profession for this figure as casually as his narrator claims Holgrave chose it, merely a passing interest and a chance for employment. In 1851, the daguerreotype represented a bold, new invention, and Hawthorne uses it to combine and confuse ancient witchcraft with futuristic technology.

Today we think of the daguerreotype as the early form of the photograph. Undoubtedly, the first led directly to the creation of the second, but when Hawthorne was writing, the jury was still out on the historical consequences of photography. Many prominent New Englanders ridiculed the invention in the 1840s, while others called it the single greatest invention that they had witnessed in their lives.

The French government announced the invention of the daguerreotype in 1839, through the work of Louis-Jacques-Mande' Daguerre, amid intense excitement and anticipation. Daguerre's book, explaining the process of fixing an image in print, was published in twenty-six editions, and translated before the end of the year! American newspapers printed some of the details, but the delicate combination of chemicals was too complicated for most readers to even attempt it. Daguerre and some of his students gave mass presentations on the difficult process. Audiences were clearly as impressed by the seemingly magical effect of capturing light patterns on a glass plate as they were by the often blurry end result. Within a short time, however, other industrious inventors were hard at work simplifying the steps and making the product more widely available. By the mid 1840s, photography was already being widely practiced. By the time of Hawthorne's publication, photographic portraits were common enough that he could

I KNOW THE FACE, FOR ITS STERN EYE HAS BEEN FOLLOWING ME ABOUT ALL DAY. IT IS MY PURITAN ANCESTOR, COLONEL PYNCHEON, WHOSE PORTRAIT HANGS IN THE PARLOR. BUT YOU HAVE GIVEN HIM MODERN DRESS.

parody the "miniatures" and assume that readers would understand him. In *The House of the Seven Gables*, Hawthorne advances a fascinating interpretation of vision (literally how people see) in relation to the new technology of photography. Holgrave and Phoebe argue over the value of daguerreotypes versus painted portraits. Phoebe says that she finds them unattractive and almost unfair to their subjects: "they are so hard and stern; besides dodging away from the eye, and trying to escape altogether. They are conscious of looking very unamiable, I suppose, and therefore hate to be seen." That she suggests a distaste of being seen on the part of the picture rather than the *person* pictured is interesting enough, but Holgrave picks up on her idea of "looking very unamiable." Phoebe assumes that people are naturally amiable, and anything that makes them seem otherwise must be unnatural, hence the desire to "escape" from the camera. On the other hand, Holgrave assumes that the "unamiable" aspect that the daguerreotype brings out is the "truth" below the superficial surface of politeness and charm. According to Holgrave, the photograph is a scientific way of detecting the hidden elements of one's character. He tells Phoebe that the light of day only illuminates "the merest surface, it actually brings out the secret character with a truth that no painter would venture upon, even could he detect it." To prove his assertions, Holgrave shows her the chemically produced image of Judge Pyncheon. She assumes that the picture is of the severe and ancient Colonel, not the seemingly jolly Judge But Holgrave corrects her and suggests that the light of "the sun tells quite another story . . . Here we have the man, sly subtle, hard, imperious, and, 'withal, cold as ice." After seeing this image, Phoebe sees the Judge's appearance as "cold [and] hard" and

...it struck Phoebe that this very Judge Pyncheon was the original which the daguerreotypist had shown her in the garden, and that the hard, stern, relentless look, now on his face, was the same that the sun had so inflexibly persisted in bringing out. Was it, therefore, no momentary mood, but, however skillfully concealed, the settled temper of his life?

So Phoebe, like Holgrave, comes to view the the photograph as a form of vision that is even more reliable than her own eyes. The Judge can conceal his truly evil intentions from her eyes, but not from those of the camera. Holgrave knows only too well how deceptive one's external identity can be; like the Judge, he too is hiding his inner self from the world. The difference for the story is that Holgrave's secret identity is that of a hero and a lover, while Judge Pyncheon is hiding his malice toward Clifford and Hepzibah.

lady." Holgrave, thinking of her courage in defying tradition, calls her "heroic."

Whether you view Hepzibah as a relic of the past or the (in the end) redeemed promise of a future free from ancestral guilt, she undoubtedly represents Hawthorne's sense that the privilege of the American upper classes would be less and less easy to inherit without the responsibilities of that power and wealth.

Clifford Pyncheon is Hepzibah's brother and a nephew of the Pyncheon who lived in the House before her. When his uncle is found murdered, Clifford's ambitious cousin Jaffrey manages to cast suspicion on Clifford. While Clifford goes to prison for the murder, Jaffrey inherits the family fortune (handing over the House to Hepzibah in the process). Clifford's long awaited return from jail occurs soon after the story begins.

Clifford is, perhaps, the most complicated (and contradictory) character in the entire book. Unlike all the others, he does not easily fit the mold of any particular type of literary figure (hero, villain, idealist, sinner, saint, etc.). Until near the end of the story, he's a lethargic, sickly victim of Jaffrey's wrongdoing. But even after thirty years of imprisonment, Clifford's early artistic sense remains. Phoebe's presence in the house brightens Clifford almost immediately, and his remarkable transformation at the end of the novel suggests that his "true" character (the intelligent, active man that his sister remembers) has been resting quietly, beneath the surface, all the time.

Phoebe Pyncheon is a cousin of Hepzibah and Clifford's and one of the last remaining members of the family. She visits Hepzibah in order to start a new life for herself, but she quickly finds herself helping the elderly siblings repair their lives. Symbolically (and rather simplistically), Phoebe plays the role of the bright (the narrator literally refers to her as bringing light into the dungeon of a house), idealistic young woman who grows through her experiences with her cousins.

Early critics and readers were fascinated by Phoebe's luminescence. **Some of the contemporary reviews of *The House of the Seven Gables* refer to the young girl as the most charming aspect of the work** More recent readers have been troubled by the gender stereotype that she fits so neatly.

It is impossible to explain how the neighborhood became aware of the girl's presence, but soon there was a great run of custom.

One might emphasize the ways in which Phoebe intelligently finagles her way into Hepzibah's good graces or her effect on Clifford as evidence of her importance to the story and her positive qualities as a character. On the other hand, Phoebe is (as the author does not hesitate to point out) highly conservative by nature. She's intuitively suspicious of Holgrave's good intentions *and* Judge Jaffrey Pyncheon's evil scheming.

tive of Hawthorne's notions of women in general, or as a parody of them, she's a compelling figure. It's also noteworthy that the novel comes to its climax while Phoebe is absent from the House—as if the death which precipitates so much change and revelation for Hepzibah and Clifford could not happen while Phoebe's "conservative" influence is close by.

Holgrave the Daguerreotypist is the paradoxically quiet radical who rents a room from Hepzibah. At the beginning of the story, the narrator presents Holgrave as a cynical social critic whose one redeeming quality is his kindness to Hepzibah. As the novel progresses, Holgrave appears to hold various types of secret information. In the novel (though the Classics Illustrated adaptation omits it), he tells Phoebe the story of Maule's curse with more detail than anyone else seems to know. *Although he claims to have fictionalized it, we have to wonder why one who claims only to want to "observe" the stage of the world has such a keen interest in this particular family's history.*

Holgrave is an observer in many ways. As a daguerreotypist, he makes photo-portraits. But he's also genuinely fascinated by the people around him. He not only makes pictures, he analyzes them as well. He points out to Phoebe the current Judge's stunning resemblance to the long-dead Colonel Pyncheon. He claims that the discovery of this resemblance is an example of the significance of the daguerreotype. Although all those who see the Judge in person see him as a pleasant, affable

man, Holgrave and Phoebe know him to be cruel. The portrait brings out the Judge's hard features in a way—Holgrave suggests—that neither a painting, nor the man himself could.

But Holgrave is only a daguerreotypist as a temporary means of making money. While this profession constitutes the "present phrase" of his life, the author gives no indication that it will be "more permanent, than any of the preceding" employments: Holgrave is an adventurer. Hawthorne has been criticized for making Holgrave a magnetic character (everyone seems to be drawn to him, including the readers!) who changes his mind and his philosophy at the drop of a hat. We meet him as a social activist and a socialist (views Phoebe considers questionable), then we find him to be an individualist (with echoes of the major American philosophers of Hawthorne's day), but, at the end of the work, he reverses himself, announcing that he's a conservative much like Phoebe. While these rapid ideological shifts make Holgrave seem inconsistent, his unyielding observation of Hepzibah and Clifford seems to point in yet another direction.

Holgrave's most startling piece of secret information is his real identity.

IF MAULE'S GHOST, OR A DESCENDANT OF HIS, COULD SEE ME NOW, HE WOULD BE WELL PLEASED.

Salem History and the Witch Trials

Although we know the Salem Witch Trials from more recent dramatizations (such as Arthur Miller's play, *"The Crucible"*) and movies, Hawthorne's use of historical events and people is an easily overlooked part of *The House of the Seven Gables*. Although the main characters inhabit the same time period as the 1851 book, their ancestors' actions in the seventeenth century provide an important backdrop to their lives.

Hawthorne combines two important historical conflicts that took place in Salem, Massachusetts, to form the prehistory of his own fiction. Both conflicts—witch trials and religious persecutions—suggest that the majority of Salem allowed a number of injustices to be committed in the name of their religion. Matthew Maule's execution clearly refers to the witchcraft trials of 1692. Maule's prophecy that "God will give" Colonel Pyncheon "blood to drink" has a historical parallel in one of the actual hangings. According to a nineteenth Century historian, one of the women, who was being hung as a witch, cursed her accuser in almost identical words. In all, twenty people were executed and approximately 400 accused of sorcery during the panic.

The other historical event is the continuous persecution of Quakers by Salem's most prominent religious leaders, throughout the second half of the seventeenth century. Hawthorne researched Salem history in the period before he wrote *The House of the Seven Gables*, and he clearly knew with whom his sympathies lay. His unappealing representation of the town might make one read the conclusion of the story—when all of the major characters (Pyncheons and Maules alike) bid "a final, glad farewell to the abode of their forefathers, with hardly more emotion than if they had made it their arrangements to return thither at tea-time." Little wonder, then, that Hawthorne himself abandoned Salem in 1850 (a year before *The House* was published) for the Berkshires!

He unmasks himself as a descendent of Matthew Maule, which both explains his obsession with the Pyncheon family and provides a way for him to solve their financial distress: he finds the long-lost deed to the Pyncheon lands. Holgrave's identity makes Hepzibah's early fantasies about an unknown savior emerging from a family connection seem ironic: in the end she is saved, not by an unknown family member, but by a member of the very family that had once cursed hers!

Judge Jaffrey Pyncheon is, of course, the villain in *The House of the Seven Gables*. No mere con-man, the Judge's greatest weapon is his affability and superficial charm. A quick-thinker, Jaffrey turns a sticky situation (being involved in the death of his uncle) to his advantage by framing his cousin Clifford. Over time, Jaffrey takes up law—one example of rather heavy-handed irony on

I REJOICE TO HEAR SO FAVORABLE A REPORT OF CLIFFORD. MANY YEARS AGO, I HAD GREAT AFFECTION FOR HIM. HEAVEN GRANT HE HAS REPENTED OF HIS PAST SINS.

NOBODY, I FANCY, COULD HAVE FEWER TO REPENT OF.

the author's part—and builds up a respectable reputation in the community. Well-known and well-liked, **the Judge is ready to threaten the only-recently released Clifford with another imprisonment unless he can lead Jaffrey to the lost deed for more**

Pyncheon lands.

On the brink of success, the Judge dies the sudden, solitary death of the Pyncheon family curse. To make his end even more parallel with the past, Judge Jaffrey Pyncheon dies in the very "ancestral" chair in which Colonel Pyncheon himself died. Readers since Hawthorne's day have hotly debated how the Judge died. One theory holds that he was so struck by the ghostly vision of Clifford that he suffered a massive heart attack. Another suggestion points to Holgrave, who could easily have killed the Judge after Hepzibah and Clifford left and before Phoebe returned. A medical explanation might point to hereditary heart disease and an inexplicable, spontaneous attack (in fact, that's what the CI adaptation implies).

Uncle Venner is (another irony) one of the few characters in the novel *not* related to either the Pyncheons or the Maules. This kindly old man is the neighborhood character.

Although generally thought to be weak minded, Uncle Venner has gained the town's respect as one who has, at least, survived into old age. His folksy wisdom and kindness cheer Hepzibah on many occasions and he's the first to recognize Phoebe's value to the resident of the House of the Seven Gables.

Little **Ned Higgins** makes only a few appearances in the story as "one of the staunchest patrons" of Hepzibah's cent store. In addition to being the store's first customer, Ned plays an important (if subtle) role in the story by pointing to some of the less felicitous

aspects of New England society. He identifies the gingerbread man that he desires as "that Jim Crow there, in the window...the one that has not a broken foot." Naming the cookie, Ned refers obliquely to the set of Jim Crow laws segregating African Americans and whites in Northern American cities. In Hepzibah's first sale, the narrator connects her shame ("an irreparable ruin") in falling from aristocrat to capitalist, with the item she has just sold, **"the impish figure of the negro dancer."** In another odd cultural reference, the book describes the boy as a "little cannibal" as he rapidly consumes one gingerbread man after another.

A LITTLE LATER, HEPZIBAH HAD HER FIRST CUSTOMER.

I WANT THAT GINGERBREAD MAN IN THE WINDOW—THE ONE THAT HAS NOT THE BROKEN FOOT.

Interestingly, Hawthorne's friend, Herman Melville—another major writer of the day and a self-described chronicler of "cannibals"—wrote to the author in a post-script: "If you pass Hepzibah's cent-shop, buy me a Jim Crow (fresh) and send it to me by Ned Higgins."

Inhabiting Land, Inheriting a Curse

In his "Preface" to *The House of the Seven Gables*, Hawthorne made a famous distinction between two literary genres, the Romance and the Novel (in a Romance, such as *House*, a reader must allow the author "a certain latitude" in its portrayal of

Themes

reader must allow the author "a certain latitude" in its portrayal of "truths"). But Hawthorne makes another distinction in the "Preface" that is worth noting as well. Some stories have a moral at the center, he suggests, and others do not. This "Tale" does have a moral, that wealthy inheritances can't conceal the crimes that originally created the wealth. So the argument of the work is that "the wrong-doing of one generation lives into the successive ones, and ... becomes a pure and uncontrollable mischief."

This *uncontrollable* mischief fascinated Hawthorne and he was convinced that the "avalanche" of "ill-gotten gold, or real estate" would eventually return all stolen items to their rightful owners. The unfair inheritance of land preoccupied the author: almost a decade before *The House of the Seven Gables*, he sketched a familiar-sounding idea for a character in one of his Notebooks: "A young girl inherits a family grave-yard—that being all that remains of rich hereditary possessions."

Inheritance was the primary way wealth was acquired in the 18th- and 19th-century United States. Families often passed down the same house from generation to generation, and with the house often came large estates of land and property. One might grow up and grow old in the same house as one's great-grandparents. Living in a house once occupied by ancestors one had never met made the idea of inheritance an inherently ghostly one.

The Past is always present in this book, whether through the characters (especially Judge Pyncheon) or through this idea of continual inheritance. Hawthorne was troubled by the idea of passing down not just money and land but ideas and values as well. In lines that echo in the 20th-century, he wrote (in Notebook entries from 1844) that he wanted

To represent the influence which Dead Men have among living affairs—for instance [in wills], a Dead Man controls the disposition of wealth .... Dead Men's opinions in all things control the living truth; we believe in Dead Men's religion ... everywhere and in all matters, Dead Men tyrannize inexorably over us

In *House*, Holgrave's views seem to come closest to representing Hawthorne's on this subject, when he tells Phoebe, "what slaves we are to bygone times." Holgrave views the process of inheritance as ensuring that "we live in Dead Men's houses; as, for instance, in this of the seven gables." Phoebe is, of course, not nearly so troubled by this point. Holgrave's perspective on this entire subject, however, changes once we find out that he's not merely a passive observer of the house, but an active participant in both its past and future.

The Role of the Past

Tradition and the burden of the past play overwhelming roles in *The House of the Seven Gables*, but not just through the process of inheritance.

THE PYNCHEONS LIVED FOR MORE THAN 150 YEARS, AND MAULE'S CURSE REMAINED A PART OF THE FAMILY INHERITANCE. IF A PYNCHEON DID BUT CLEAR HIS THROAT,

HE HAS MAULE'S BLOOD TO DRINK.

Almost all of Hawthorne's characters mirror past people or events. This sense of the present repeating and reenacting the past is an important theme for the author.

The Judge is the most obvious (and least attractive) representative of the past. His physical resemblance to the Colonel and their almost identical deaths—not to mention all of the strange deaths in between—suggest that the present moment is nothing but an uncanny echo of the past. The theme of witchcraft, and the seriousness with which the novel takes it, **closely links the 1850 setting of the main story to the 1690s of the characters's ancestors.** Similarly, a few of the minor characters, such as Uncle Venner, could appear in a novel from almost any period of U.S. literature.

However, the major characters refer to the past while giving it a more modern twist. Hepzibah's ancient appearance, her obsessions with "antique portraits, pedigrees, coats of arms, records,

and traditions," and her aristocratic shame at opening a cent shop link her to the family's (and the nation's) past. At the same time, she *does* open the shop, and makes her first sale to young Ned, one of the few references to the town's future. As Uncle Venner reminds her, she always has the (disagreeable, yet available) option of asking Judge Pyncheon for money. But rather than bow to him, she opens the shop and (with the aid of Phoebe's charm) begins to make it a success.

Similarly, Clifford is a character who both points to the past and transforms the present. By nature and as a result of being imprisoned for thirty years, he's "the most inveterate of conservatives."

Who Killed Judge Pyncheon? And When? (And Why?)

Critics have argued the question of the Judge's death for decades without any clear resolution. Some readers say that Holgrave must have killed him, while others have found reasons to suspect Clifford, Phoebe, the unnamed narrator, Hepzibah, and almost every other possible character except maybe Ned. Without any way of knowing for sure, we might find it more useful to ask *why* we want to pin the death on one specific character's actions. *What will it tell us about the work to know who killed the villain?*

In an influential 1956 essay, critic Alfred H. Marks argued that natural causes—a "hereditary liability" that created a mortal (and entirely internal) attack—were not convincing enough as a final answer. As an alternative, Marks points out that Clifford must be the first

NOW THE JUDGE'S OWN DEATH, IN THE SAME SUDDEN WAY, IS A PUNISHMENT FOR HIS WICKEDNESS, AND MAKES PLAIN CLIFFORD'S INNOCENCE.

actually in the same room as the Judge. It seems reasonable to consider that Clifford's pale, ghostly appearance before the "weary" Judge could have itself caused him such a violent shock that he died on the spot. Remember that the Judge had not seen Clifford since before his thirty years in prison (for the Judge's crime). The argument, in sum, is that the death, like the novel itself, is a product of imagination. Judge Jaffrey's imagination overtakes him when he thinks he sees, not Clifford, but Clifford's *ghost* haunting him.

Others point accusatory fingers at Holgrave. Couldn't this mysterious man have stolen into the room while the Judge waited impatiently for Clifford and killed him? Phoebe seems shocked that Holgrave could have seen the dead body and taken a picture of it rather than going to the authorities. His delay casts suspicion on Holgrave, but one would have to wonder why he would do it. Even his secret identity as a Maule does not explain Holgrave's motive, since only he knows where the family land deeds are. Under other circumstances he could easily have bargained with Judge Pyncheon to get the deeds.

Some see the events of Jaffrey Pyncheon's death in terms of Hawthorne's biography, as a comment on the relationships in his own life; and some, as a philosophical statement on the ways in which guilt acts like a parasite, killing those who allow it to nest within them.

Ultimately, the crucial point seems to be that we do not know for sure who was with the Judge when he died. The narration leaves the room with the Judge calmly waiting; when it returns to the room, he is dead.

Possessions

The idea of "possession" is the governing metaphor of *The House of the Seven Gables*. On one level, the plot of the story follows two families, the Maules and the Pyncheons, dueling over the possession of land. This was (and is) a common enough vehicle for a story about the effect of conflict over many generations.

But possession has other meanings. Fears of witchcraft can be best described as concern that another person will *possess* one's mind and soul. Although the CI adaptation omits it, Holgrave interrupts the novel to insert his fanciful version of the story of Alice Pyncheon, the daughter of the Colonel. In Holgrave's telling, young Matthew Maule (grandson of the executed wizard) uses the Colonel's insatiable greed to his own advantage. In describing Maule, Holgrave reports that the popular wisdom of the day held that the grandson had "inherited some of his ancestor's questionable traits" and that he might even be able to control others.

He was fabled, for example, to

ve a strange power of getting into
...ople's dreams, and regulating matters
...there according to his own fancy, pretty
much like the stage-manager of a the-
ater. . . . Some said, that he could look
into people's minds; others, that . . . he
could draw people into his own mind.

However ominously the story begins, it soon lives up to its own hints. Maule offers to try to tell the Colonel where the lost deeds to his lands are, if the Colonel will let him speak to his daughter. Thinking more about material possessions than spiritual or emotional, the father agrees. Although (or because) Alice feels herself to be "impenetrable" in her own power, Maule puts her into a hypnotic trance. Unable to revive his daughter, the Colonel speaks of her as he might of a possession: "You . . . have robbed me of my daughter! Give her back—spawn of the old wizard!—or you shall climb Gallows-Hill in your grandfather's footsteps!" Maule does awaken Alice, but only to prove to her father that he has entirely possessed her soul.

And there is yet another form of possession in *The House.* Holgrave, the daguerreotypist, captures and then prints images (usually portraits) as an employment. His daguerreotypes play an important role in the plot by pointing out (usually to Phoebe) the "true" nature of those portrayed. Unlike the painting of Colonel Pyncheon, Holgrave's portraits reflect not the outward character that the subject wants

to show others, but that which the subject attempts to hide. Thus, when Phoebe sees the daguerreotype of the Judge, she assumes from the severity of the face that it is of his ancestor, the Colonel. Similarly, Phoebe learns from one of Holgrave's images that the Judge is dead, not from seeing his actual body.

Finally, of course, the plot resolves itself in making known all of the secrets that Matthew Maule has kept hidden He recovers the documents from the hiding-spot that has held them for years upon years. More importantly, he reveals his love to Phoebe and his identity as a member of the Maule family. Through this

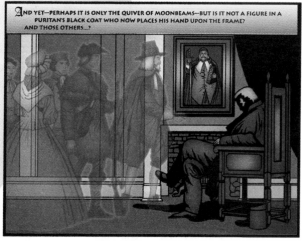

AND YET—PERHAPS IT IS ONLY THE QUIVER OF MOONBEAMS—BUT IS IT NOT A FIGURE IN A PURITAN'S BLACK COAT WHO NOW PLACES HIS HAND UPON THE FRAME? AND THOSE OTHERS...?

kinship with the early Maules, Holgrave breaks the ancient curse on the Pyncheon family and puts Hepzibah and Clifford in possession of their own destiny.

•What is the proof of inheritance and why is evidence so important? Would it change

•What is the proof of inheritance and why is evidence so important? Would it change the story significantly if Judge Pyncheon had found the deeds before he died? How so?

•Only the Pyncheons show up in pictures in *The House*. What would a daguerreotype of *Holgrave* reveal about him? Would it show his secret identity as a Maule? Would it suggest positive or negative characteritics? How?

•Is the neat and tidy conclsion of *The House of the Seven Gables* entirely convincing? Or might it be a satire on novels with perfectly resolved endings? Are all of the conflicts within the story really resolved? Does the ending make sense with the rest of the novel, or are there inconsistecies?

•Henry James, one of the foremost U.S. authors of the late 19th and early 20th-centuries, wrote that Hawthorne was an especially "American" writer in that he felt the urge "to keep analyzing and cunningly considering" the past. How does Hawthorne analyze and consider the past in *The House in the Seven Gables*? Can you think of other American authors who depict the past in their fiction? Why might authors choose to portray the past when they could show the same actions in their own time?

•Why might Hawthorne have left the Judge's death so unclear? Is it significant that he is sitting underneath the portrait of Colonel Pyncheon? Why does Holgrave seem to suggest both natural causes ("physical predisposition") and divine judgment (it "seems the stroke of God upon him ... a punishment for his wickedness") at the same time? Which do you think it was?

About the Essayist:

Joshua Miller is an Instructor in the Department of English and Comparative Literature at Columbia University. He holds an M.Phil degree from Columbia.